DESIGNING PLAYGROUNDS

Math Projects Series

JAN HAM

DALE SEYMOUR PUBLICATIONS

Pearson Learning Group

To Kevin

Managing Editor: Catherine Anderson
Production/Manufacturing Director: Janet Yearian
Design Manager: Jeff Kelly
Project Editor: Joan Gideon
Senior Production Coordinator: Alan Noyes
Art: Rachel Gage and Penny Carson
Composition: Brandon Carson
Text and cover design: Polly Christensen, Christensen & Son Design

Playgrounds shown on pages 14, 32, 37, 42, 43, 48–51 are courtesy of KOMPAN, Inc., Seattle, Washington.
Playgrounds shown on pages 38, and 44–47 are courtesy of R. Hagelberg, Olympic Recreation, Gary, Indiana.
Playground shown on pages 52 and 53 is courtesy of Pentes Play, Inc., Charlotte, North Carolina.

ISBN 1-57232-275-6
Printed in the United States of America
5 6 7 8 9 10   07 06 05 04 03

QA
135.5
.H36
1998

Dale
Seymour
Publications

Pearson Learning Group

1-800-321-3106
www.pearsonlearning.com

◆◇ CONTENTS ◆◇

◆◆ INTRODUCTION ◆◆

FROM THE FIRST EXPLORATIONS OF HOME, NEIGH-borhood, and the world beyond, a young child appraises each new space in terms of play. A fallen tree, an overturned wheelbarrow, or a gate (things adults barely give a second glance) become things to climb up, hide under, or swing on. The child discovers architecture—the columns flanking the courthouse doors, the curved space of an attic turret room, the cool space beneath the porch stairs—and asks, "What can I turn this space into? What can I play here?"

Students in grades 5 through 8 are not so far out of childhood as to forget how to invent play spaces, which makes them excellent playground designers.

Architectural Design Education

Architectural design, which includes designing playgrounds, makes mathematics less abstract and more real. Students use geometry and measurement for authentic, hands-on tasks of spatial inquiry. The design process includes

- Define a design problem
- Conceptualize a solution
- Construct and test models
- Evaluate that solution
- Present that solution to others

Through architectural design education, students

- make connections within and across disciplines (math, science, history, writing, and art)
- solve open-ended problems in more than one way
- work as cooperating members of design teams
- create, control, and make decisions about the built environment
- recognize architecture as technology, art, a

means for solving human problems, and an expression of human ideas

The National Council of Teachers of Mathematics' *Curriculum and Evaluation Standards for School Mathematics* (page 50) states, "Perhaps the most important connection to be fostered in mathematics instruction is the connection between the mathematical ideas and students' experience within a real-world context." For your students, designing playgrounds is the real world.

As they work through the activities in this book, your students will use skills in mathematics (geometry, measurement, estimating, and scale), science (materials and engineering), and social studies (surveys, contracts, community planning, and social interaction) to clearly express their ideas about space and about play.

For the final project, students will plan, design, and build a model of a playground. In real life, the client reviews the park or building before spending money for construction. In the same way, your students will present and defend their projects.

This is a kid-tested, hands-on, use-real-playgrounds curriculum. Plan on doing this book in a season suited to outdoor activities. If they cannot work outside, students can accomplish a lot in the school gym. If you do not have much of a playground at your school, arrange a field trip to one nearby.

The sequence of activities requires 11 to 12 classroom hours. To run a seven-hour sequence, you can do just activities 1, 2, 5, 6, 7, 9, and the final project.

If you expand these projects into other parts of your curriculum, allow more time. You don't need to work on them every day, but once a week is not often enough. Three times a week works well. Where will you find the time? Most teachers use their math time; some use other curriculum-related time as well. If it is a particularly nice day out, teachers find that extra time to work outside.

Some Suggestions

In the first activity, students create design folders in which to keep their sketches and handouts. These folders can serve as students' design notebooks for the planning lists, surveys, evaluations, and notes needed in subsequent planning sessions. Design notebooks are also good places for students to periodically write paragraphs in which they reflect on their learning.

You may modify the blackline masters by taping sections of typed questions or instructions over master copies. You may also make calculations simpler or more complex in this way.

Most students need to spend extra time on the practical art of measuring things. Do not just talk about square footage, get out on the playground with yardsticks and string. Students should have skills from a basic or refresher geometry unit and understand measurement before they begin designing.

If students are having trouble describing something with words or on paper (such as what a climbing rope looks like drawn from above), remember to communicate spatially. Dangle a piece of string and have students look at it from above.

Giving students access to a box of common model-making materials (spools, sticks, pipe cleaners, toy tires, and so on) helps them and you. Instead of interpreting your students' visions for them, you are helping them find their own ways of communicating their ideas. For example, a student envisions stairs leading up to a platform. He knows what is in his mind, but says he can not draw it. If you have him make a simple model (an accordion-folded strip of paper for stairs and an upside-down cherry tomato basket for the platform), the chances are very good he will be able to draw it on his own.

Suggest often that students collect their own materials, as their final projects will include model playgrounds built at home.

Take photographs and videos of this year's projects, and save sample plans and models to inspire next year's students.

Enlist an art teacher's help in clarifying the difference between drawing in perspective (where things appear to get smaller as they get farther away from you) and drawing an architectural plan, which someone can measure and use while building the structure.

Materials

Paper

The activities use a scale of $\frac{1}{4}$ inch equals 1 foot so students can fit a playground design on an 11- by 17-inch piece of grid paper. Although paper is rectangular, allow students to design nonrectangular playgrounds. For example, they can tape paper together or cut out circles for interesting site shapes.

- $\frac{1}{4}$-inch grid paper (8 $\frac{1}{2}$- by 11-inch size) or use copies of the $\frac{1}{4}$-inch grid paper blackline master on page 59
- $\frac{1}{4}$-inch grid paper (11- by 17-inch size) or tape together 2 copies of the $\frac{1}{4}$-inch grid paper blackline master on page 59
- 8 $\frac{1}{2}$- by 11-inch tracing paper
- at least 10 sheets of 11- by 17-inch tracing paper or a roll of 18-inch architect's canary tracing paper
- notebook or folder for each student (for holding drawings, surveys, and design notes, called the *design notebook*)
- lined paper for notebooks (10 to 15 sheets per student)
- easel with 6 or more poster-size sheets of paper

Copies and Transparencies

This list of blackline masters indicates which pages to turn into transparencies and which you will need to copy for each student. (You may want to run them off all at once.)

- What Actions? (1 per student)
- Bodies in Space (1 per student)
- Children's Play Survey (2 per student, optional transparency)
- String Math (1 per student)
- Sample Site (1 per student)

- From Perspective to Plan (1 per student, transparency)
- Sample Plan (1 per student, transparency)
- Sample Playgrounds 1–7 (transparencies)
- Plan Template and Elevation Template (1 each per student, transparencies)
- Space Needs for Wheelchair Use (transparency)
- Evaluation (2 per student)
- Contract (2 per student, transparency)
- Triangle Paper (several colors and sizes per student, transparencies)
- Final Project (1 per student)
- $\frac{1}{4}$-inch grid paper (as needed to replace pads of grid paper, transparency)

Tools and Supplies

The activities tell you how and when to use each of these following items.

- timer or stopwatch
- glue
- drafting tape (looks like masking tape, but comes off of paper and desks easily)
- stapler
- string (200 feet or more)
- video camera (optional)

per team of 2 students

- at least one measuring tape (preferably 25 feet) or a yardstick
- tape and glue

per team of 4 students

- builder's chalk line (handy, but optional)
- 2 or more pieces of chalk in 2 colors
- 18-foot piece of string
- four 12-foot ropes
- 2 or more sample square feet (12- by 12-inch squares of cardboard or laminated grid paper)

per student

- 6-inch pipe cleaner (optional)
- sharp pencil (or mechanical pencils) with erasers
- ruler with clear markings to $\frac{1}{4}$-inch
- clipboard for outdoor activities
- drafting triangle, such as an 8-inch, 45-degree plastic triangle (optional)
- compass or other circle-drawing tool
- penny
- scissors

Model-Making Supplies

Use any math manipulatives you have. Also collect common supplies as you discover free or inexpensive sources for them. Ask students to bring recycled materials from home.

- math manipulatives: pattern blocks, geometric solids, 1-inch square tiles, tangram pieces, linking cubes, Cuisenaire® rods, and so on
- toy houses, toy cars, toy animals
- small toy people about 1 inch high
- cardboard cylinders, cones, and small plain boxes
- empty film canisters and thread spools
- wooden blocks
- toy tires or hole reinforcers for tires
- toy ladders
- Styrofoam or plastic packaging that looks architectural, such as cherry-tomato baskets, cookie trays, or packing bubbles
- straws, string, paper clips, pipe cleaners, twist-ties, ice cream sticks, toothpicks
- colored acetate

Visual Samples

Collect photographs of playgrounds, pictures from playground catalogs, sample playground plans, and models.

◇◇ ACTIVITY SUMMARY ◇◇

Activity	Time	Transparencies
1. Natural Play, Playground Play	30 minutes	What Actions?
2. Bodies in Space	20 minutes	
3. Children's Play Survey	two 30-minute sessions	Children's Play Survey (optional)
4. Site Shapes	45 minutes	
5. Plans, Elevations, and Scale	two 45-minute sessions	Sample Playground 1 From Perspective to Plan Sample Plan Elevation Template $\frac{1}{4}$-Inch Grid Paper
6. The Design Process	30 minutes	Sample Playgrounds 1–7 Sample Plan Space Needs for Wheelchairs Plan and Elevation Templates
7. Pattern-Block Playgrounds	45 minutes	
8. Evaluating a Playground	two 45-minute sessions	
9. Designing from Contracts	two 45-minute sessions	Contract
10. Three-Dimensional Models	45 minutes	Triangle Paper $\frac{1}{4}$-Inch Grid Paper
Final Project	two 45-minute sessions plus 60 minutes for presentations	

Activity	*What Students Do*
1. Natural Play, Playground Play	• generate Actions List; copy it into notebooks • complete What Actions? worksheet
2. Bodies in Space	• measure another student to complete Bodies in Space worksheet
3. Children's Play Survey	• observe children on playground to complete Children's Play Survey • write Survey Results in notebooks
4. Site Shapes	• draw chalk squares and grids on pavement • complete String Math worksheet • make string outlines of Sample Site
5. Plans, Elevations, and Scale	• complete From Perspective to Plan worksheet • make scale figures out of pipe cleaners • trace Sample Plan • trace elevations from template
6. The Design Process	• create Design Process list in notebooks during class discussion
7. Pattern-Block Playgrounds	• make two-dimensional playground plan
8. Evaluating a Playground	• draw plan and elevation of playground piece • evaluate playground using Evaluation worksheet
9. Designing from Contracts	• fill out Contract and design site • trace parts from Plan Template and Elevation Template to create playground • analyze cost of playground • submit plan and Contract to reviewer
10. Three-Dimensional Models	• cut, fold, and tape Triangle Paper and grid paper to make three-dimensional shapes • combine shapes into class playground model
Final Project	• perform all aspects of designing a playground using Final Project, Evaluation, and Contract worksheets

Natural Play, Playground Play

Playing on a playground is fun, but it also stimulates physical, social, and intellectual learning. Play is pretending, trying out future roles, inventing new games, solving problems, learning about gravity and motion, and testing limits. What are students' definitions of play?

Time. 30 minutes
Place. classroom

Materials

- photographs, catalog pages, and plans of playgrounds
- stapler
- easel with paper
- Sample Playground 7 transparency (optional)

per student

- notebook
- 5 sheets of lined paper
- What Actions?

Preparation

- Make a transparency of Sample Playground 7 (page 52, optional).
- Make copies of What Actions? (page 32).
- Post photographs, catalog pages, and plans of playgrounds around the classroom.
- Have each student create a design notebook by stapling five sheets of paper to the inside of a folder or putting them into a notebook.

Class Discussion

Before there were playgrounds, there were trees, fields, rocks, streams, and caves—a marvelous, diverse landscape for climbing, swinging, and hiding. Playgrounds were invented as more and more children began to grow up in cities with less and less space. In the 1880s, the idea that began in Germany as sand gardens was brought to America. Boston's Charlesbank Park contained iron frames and ladders, swings, teeter-totters, climbing ropes, and poles. Modern playgrounds are necessary and safe, but how well do they replace contact with nature? Just how jungle-like is a jungle gym?

Playground designers know that children's play becomes more creative and open-ended on playgrounds that include natural settings. Ask a child why she chose the fallen tree limb over a plastic imitation, and she may simply say it was a better place to hide. Designers understand that trees offer more loose materials to manipulate (branches to arrange), and that "environmental modification to create enclosed spaces is high on the list of preferred activities for children." (MaryAnn Kirby. "Nature as Refuge in Children's Environments." *Children's Environments Quarterly*, Spring 1989, p. 7.)

Creating an Actions List

As you discuss where and how children play outside, today and in the past, draw three columns on the easel paper and label them *Actions*, *Natural Site*, and *Playground*.

1. Write the word *field* at the top of the Natural Site column. Have students help you add to this list of things in nature they can play on or in (such as rocks, trees, and streams).

Actions	Natural Site	Playground
run, chase, leapfrog, . . .	field	open space
slide, climb, roll, . . .	hill	slide
climb, swing, fall, . . .	tree	jungle gym
balance, jump over, cross, . . .	logs	balance beam
fly, swing, climb, . . .	vines	ropes
hide, seek, crawl, . . .	cave	tunnel
watch	stream, pond, . . .	
pretend, build	sand, snow	
compete for territory	big rocks, . . .	
get dizzy		
ride		

2. Ask students to name action words that describe what one person or more could play on an open field. Write these words in the Action column across from the word *field*. Continue listing action words for all of the natural sites listed.

3. For the Playground column, have students tell you which playground pieces relate to an element in nature, pieces on which they can do the same actions. For example, they can hide in a natural cave or a man-made playground tunnel.

Have students copy this chart into their design notebooks and title it "Actions List."

Students can complete the What Actions? worksheet in class or as homework. For the class discussion, ask students to suggest actions that would occur on each of the three play sites and the title they would give that play site. Sample Playground 7 (page 52) is a very elaborate play structure with lots of unusual areas. You may want to show it now and talk about the names of the pieces (see pages 52, 53) and the actions these names suggest.

Ask students to consider each of the ten titles for play structures and describe what they imagine these might look like. As they talk about their ideas, they can sketch them on the chalkboard.

If students think of actions not already on the Actions List, add them. Save the easel list for reference in future planning sessions. Have students keep their Actions Lists and What Actions? worksheets in their design notebooks.

Bodies in Space

Students often underestimate how much space real bodies need to play. With these exercises in spatial visualizing, measuring, estimating, and drawing, students explore real space.

Time. 20 minutes

Place. classroom or outside

Materials

per team of 2 students

- measuring tape or yardstick

per student

- design notebook

- Bodies in Space

- one $8\frac{1}{2}$- by 11-inch sheet of $\frac{1}{4}$-inch grid paper

Preparation

- Make copies of Bodies in Space (page 33).

Directing the Activity

Divide students into two-member teams. Have the pairs measure each other as they follow the directions on the Bodies in Space worksheet.

The chart at the top of the worksheet shows the size of a 3-year old. Students will make the same kind of chart for someone their age. As students complete the questions at the bottom of the page, they will use the information from the chart on the worksheet to answer question 1 and the information from their chart for the other estimates and answers. Once all the students have completed the chart and estimates, go outside or to a large area to make class measurements for questions 3 and 4.

Students will use these statistics in later playground planning. Have them put their completed worksheets and drawings in their design notebooks.

◦◦ ACTIVITY 3 ◦◦

Children's Play Survey

In this activity, students talk about how children play. They make some hypotheses about the popularity of playground equipment and the different ways boys and girls play. They survey the play of some children and test their hypotheses.

Time. two 30-minute sessions

Place. playground and classroom

Materials

- timer or stopwatch
- easel with paper

per student

- pencil
- clipboard
- Children's Play Survey
- design notebook

Preparation

- Make copies of the survey (page 34).
- Make a transparency of the survey (optional).
- Find a class of younger students to serve as subjects for the survey.

Class Discussion

Ask students, "What are children's favorite places to play? Do you think young children play differently than older children? Do boys play differently than girls?"

A hypothesis is a tentative explanation that accounts for a set of facts and that can be tested by further investigation. On easel paper, write some of your students' hypotheses about how children play.

Introducing the Survey

Explain to students that they are going to be scientific observers. Each student will watch a selected subject at play (from a class of younger students). The observers will fill in their Children's Play Survey worksheets as they watch their subjects for exactly five minutes.

The boxes on the worksheet denote common playground actions and pieces. As a class, fill in the blank spaces with other actions or pieces appropriate to your playground. Each student will choose a subject. If the subject is a boy, the observer writes a *B* in the box every time the subject does the action for that box. For girls, the observer writes *Gs*. Observers may use their survey sheets for more than one subject, but they should observe only one subject at a time.

You will call out each minute as it passes. Those observers who are watching a subject doing one activity minute after minute should make a new mark in that activity box for each minute.

If a subject does a lot of different activities, the observer will have a lot of marks on the worksheet. If a subject does an activity more than once, have the observer mark each time this happens.

Do a trial run of the process first, having the class observe you or a student doing a preplanned series of activities on the playground. Check students' trial surveys in a group discussion—surveys are useful only if students are all using the same methods.

Doing the Survey

When the subjects are on the playground, have observers silently choose their first subjects. When everyone is ready, start timing five one-minute intervals. You may repeat the survey, having observers choose different subjects each time. Three subject observations per student works well.

Balance BB	Fall	Jump G	Seek	Yell
Build/Dig B G	Fight	Pretend	Slide GGG	Seesaw B

Tabulating Survey Results and Making Conclusions

For the second session (back in the classroom), use easel paper or a transparency of the survey to find the totals of how many boys climbed, how many girls jumped, and so on. Title this list "Survey Results." Ask students these questions.

- Realizing this is a small survey of a specific age group, what conclusions can we make about how children play?

- Would another survey give you greatly different results?

- How much did the play equipment influence what children did?

- How do these conclusions compare with the hypotheses we formed before we did our survey?

- How can we use these results in planning our playgrounds?

Have students copy the Survey Results in their design notebooks.

Extension. Have a small group of students visit the younger students' classroom. Have your students ask these questions, write down the replies, and report the results.

1. What is your favorite piece of playground equipment to play on?

2. If you could add one thing to the playground, what would it be and why?

3. When you are on the playground, do you ever pretend to be someone or something other than yourself? What do you pretend to be?

Exploring Site Shapes

In this activity, students use string and chalk to display geometric shapes on pavement. Using grids, they evaluate the play space of various shapes, a hill, and a stream.

Time. 45 minutes
Place. outside on pavement

Materials

- 2 long pieces of string (100 feet or longer each)
- scissors

per team of 4 students

- 2 or more pieces of chalk (in 2 colors)
- builder's chalk line (optional)
- 18-foot piece of string
- at least 1 measuring tape or yardstick
- four 12-foot measuring ropes (see Preparation)
- 40 short pieces of yarn or a marking pen
- at least 2 cardboard or grid-paper square feet

per student

- design notebook
- ruler
- String Math
- Sample Site

Preparation

- Make copies of String Math (page 35) and Sample Site (page 36).

- Have the class help you make measuring ropes—thin ropes cut to 12-foot lengths and clearly marked at each foot with a marker or tightly tied yarn.

- Divide the class into teams of four students each.

Beginning the Activity

Go over the String Math and Sample Site worksheets with the class. Clarify the process of enlarging the drawings. Each $\frac{1}{4}$- by $\frac{1}{4}$-inch block on the worksheet will become a 1- by 1-foot block of space on the pavement.

On the pavement, have each team practice making straight, visible chalk lines with the builder's chalk line or chalk and string. The string is the guide, the chalk makes the line.

Have each team use chalk and four measuring ropes to draw a 12- by 12-foot square. They should use two measuring ropes for horizontal lines and two measuring ropes for vertical lines.

To be sure the square is square, teams can measure the two diagonals, adjusting the sides until the diagonals are of equal length. If they do not have a 25-foot tape measure, they can use the long string to compare and equalize the diagonals.

Introduce the concept of *grids*. A grid is a pattern of regularly spaced horizontal and vertical lines forming squares.

Discussion. Ancient Egyptians used rope grids to lay out their fields. Romans used grids to plan their cities. Why is a grid useful to design on? Who else uses grids? What games are based on grids?

Drawing Shapes on Grids

Have each team turn its square into a grid of 1-by-1-foot blocks. The measuring ropes and the paper square-feet shapes can guide the teams. Have each student then answer questions 1 through 3 on String Math.

Next, have each team draw the shapes shown on String Math onto its grid using a contrasting chalk color. Discuss the geometry of these shapes as students work. For example, making a circle involves acting out its definition—a center point and a point revolving at a fixed distance from the center point.

Ask what those shapes could become on a real playground (the rectangle could be a slide or a bridge, the circle could be a tower or pool), and then have each student complete the questions on String Math.

Challenge. Any two children playing with a rope have probably discovered for themselves how to make a spiral, but do they know what they have created? Have teams use bodies, chalk, and string to make a spiral. Then ask teams to describe their spiral mathematically. (A spiral is a curve on a plane that continuously winds around a fixed point at an increasing or decreasing distance.)

Exploring the Sample Site

On a clear expanse of pavement or on the playing field, have the class work together to lay out, with string, the outer outline of the hill drawn on the Sample Site. Have them estimate how long a loop of string they will need, measure how wide the hill is, and then lay out the string. Explain to students that between two consecutive contour lines, the elevation rises one foot. Have the class cut a piece of string to lay out the innermost outline of the hill, the plateau that becomes the top of the hill.

Ask students to visualize how steep the hill would be. (The chart on the Sample Site indicates the hill rises 6 feet within about six feet, so the angle will be approximately 45°.) Discuss how the hill could be used as part of a playground. Similarly lay out the stream and some trees using string.

Recalling the Actions List and Children's Play Survey, discuss what children might play on this site and what man-made playground pieces could be added to these natural elements (such as a bridge across the stream, a slide down from a tree, and a lookout tower on the hill).

Challenge. Is the area of the hill larger or smaller than your classroom? How could students use the perimeter string that outlined the hill to answer this question? (Bring the string back to the classroom and see.)

Have students put the String Math and Sample Site worksheets in their design notebooks.

Plans, Elevations, and Scale

In this activity, students create *plans* (views drawn from above) of a sample playground and draw *elevations* (views from the side) of some of the pieces. They think about playground pieces and begin to analyze spaces and dimensions of a playground.

Time. two 45-minute sessions

Place. classroom

Materials

- transparencies of Sample Playground 1, From Perspective to Plan, Sample Plan, and Elevation Template

- transparency of $\frac{1}{4}$-Inch Grid Paper

- glue

- variously scaled toys such as houses, action figures, plastic animals, and toy cars

- cardboard or grid-paper square foot

- solid shapes (pattern blocks, 1-inch tiles, Cuisenaire® rods, hole reinforcers), string, and colored acetate for overhead transparency demonstration

per student

- From Perspective to Plan

- scissors

- three $8\frac{1}{2}$- by 11-inch sheets of $\frac{1}{4}$-inch grid paper

- sharpened pencil

- one 6-inch pipe cleaner or a scale figure (optional)

- drafting triangle, compass, and ruler

- drafting tape

- Sample Plan

- 2 sheets of $8\frac{1}{2}$- by 11-inch tracing paper

- Elevation Template

- design notebook

Preparation

- Make transparencies of Sample Playground 1 (page 42), From Perspective to Plan (page 37), Sample Plan (page 38), and Elevation Template (page 40). Have an overhead projector ready to use.

- Make copies of From Perspective to Plan, Sample Plan, and Elevations Template.

- Locate other playground plans, models, and model-making materials to show students.

Class Discussion

People first form ideas for playgrounds in their minds. How can they communicate their visions to others? How can they describe the playgrounds clearly enough so someone else could actually build the playgrounds? Talking or writing may be beginnings. But by drafting (drawing architectural structures in scale) or making scale models, even the most complicated of structures can be accurately described and clearly understood.

A plan is an exact but smaller drawing of a playground drawn as if looking directly down from above. An elevation is an exact but smaller drawing drawn as if looking directly across from one side.

They are two-dimensional drawings of three-dimensional objects. To accurately describe an object, you need both a plan and one or more elevations.

A plan, for example, will show the length and width of a slide but not its height. The elevation of that slide will show its height and length but not its width. A standing cylinder drawn in plan is a circle and drawn in elevation is a rectangle.

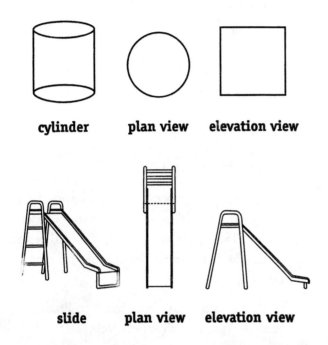

cylinder   **plan view**   **elevation view**

slide   **plan view**   **elevation view**

A perspective drawing is a three-dimensional view of an object. While perspective drawings imitate what we really see, plans and elevations more clearly indicate dimensions and proportions.

Since the goal is to make clear, buildable designs, students are to draw plans and elevations only. If their drawings start to look three-dimensional, students should redraw them. If students want to learn perspective drawing, enlist the art teacher's help in a separate session.

Make a transparency of Sample Playground 1 (page 41). Cut the pieces of the plan apart. Show the students the perspective drawing, and ask them to show you how to put the pieces together to make the plan. Show and explain the transparency From Perspective to Plan.

Have students cut the pieces from their own From Perspective to Plan worksheets and glue them

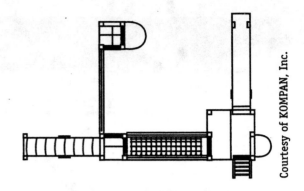

Courtesy of KOMPAN, Inc.

onto $8\frac{1}{2}$- by 11-inch grid paper to form an accurate plan of the given playground. The diagram above shows the accurate plan.

Any of the other sample playgrounds 2–6 can be used in a similar way, though it is harder to see the individual piece in a photograph.

Scale indicates just how much smaller every bit of a drawing is in relationship to the real structure. Without that indication of relative size (such as 1 inch = 1 foot or $\frac{1}{4}$ inch = 1 foot), no one can accurately imagine that structure, let alone build it.

Hand out variously scaled toy figures and discuss their scales. A figure $1\frac{1}{2}$ inches tall would represent a 6-foot person in $\frac{1}{4}$ inch = 1 foot scale. (There are 6 quarter inches in $1\frac{1}{2}$ inches.)

If students would like to use scale figures for this and following activities, now would be a good time to have students take 6-inch pipe cleaners and create small figures. Have students choose an appropriate height for the figure, such as 1 inch tall for a 4-foot child.

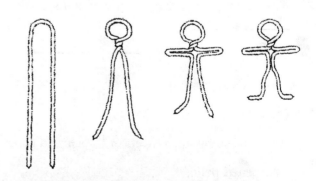

1. **Fold pipe cleaner in half.**
2. **Twist near the top to form a head.**
3. **Crimp the two ends near the head to form arms.**
4. **Bend legs to form feet so the figure measures 1 inch high.**

Using Grids to Plan Playgrounds

Overlay the Sample Plan transparency on the overhead projector with the $\frac{1}{4}$-inch grid paper transparency. Discuss how a grid can help in playground planning.

Project just the grid-paper transparency onto the chalkboard. Holding up a square foot, remind the class that each $\frac{1}{4}$-inch square on the grid will represent one square foot.

Arrange solid shapes (pattern blocks, 1-inch tiles, hole reinforcers for tires), string (for fencing), and transparent shapes (cut colored acetate) on the projected transparency grid to represent various playground pieces. Have students use the results from Bodies in Space and String Math as they do the following, individually or as a class. On $\frac{1}{4}$-inch grid paper,

- Draw specific geometric shapes for a playground plan using $\frac{1}{4}$ inch = 1 foot scale.

- Draw platforms for one person, for four people, and for eight people to stand on.

- Draw a round pool the whole class can encircle.

- Draw a walkway wide enough for two people and long enough to run on for five seconds.

- Draw the String Math circle and the triangle inside of it.

Tracing Plans and Elevations

Encourage students to maintain good drawing habits. Ask them to draw lines lightly but firmly with sharp pencils. They should use rulers or drafting triangles to draw straight lines and use compasses or circle templates to draw curves. Drafting triangles allow more accurate perpendicular and parallel lines. Drawing along two sides of the triangle, shifting it, and drawing again makes a square.

Moving along a base line and drawing along one side of the triangle makes a series of parallel lines.

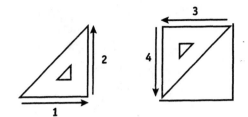

drawing a square

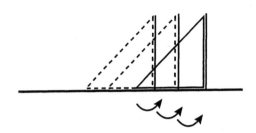

drawing parallel lines

Ask students to block print all the labels in a uniform size. Except when drawing the most preliminary of sketches, students should redraw sloppy work and use the proper tools. If you think students' ideas are worth such careful attention, they will, too.

Have students secure the Sample Plan to their desks with drafting tape (which peels off easily), then tape tracing paper on top of it. Have them trace

- title block (title, the student's name, and the scale)

- playground pieces

- labels

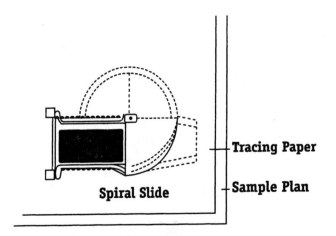

Students trace the items on the Sample Plan.

Talk about the scale of the plan. Using the transparency of the Sample Plan, show students how to add dimension lines to their tracings. A dimension line indicates the length of one side of an object. It is a double-headed arrow drawn parallel to the side of that object. The line runs the exact length of the side it is describing.

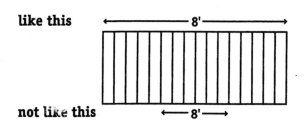

like this

not like this

Point out that the platforms on the play structure are different heights. Have students answer the questions below in a group discussion or individually as a written assignment. They can lay their tracings over blank pieces of $\frac{1}{4}$-inch grid paper. Their answers should be in real size. Each $\frac{1}{4}$ inch of the Sample Plan equals 1 foot of real space.

- How long is the tube slide? (*about 8 feet*)

- How much space is there between the clatter bridge and the chin bar? (*a little more than 9 feet*)

- How wide are the bars on the overhead ladder? (*about 2 feet 4 inches*). How far apart are the bars? (*about 16 inches*)

- What are the dimensions of the platform attached to the coil? ($3\frac{1}{2}$ *feet by 4 feet*)

- After climbing the coil, what can the child do next? (*Go up to the platform at the right and go down one of the slides or play with the wheel, or go down to the platform ahead and go across the ring trek or the clatter bridge.*)

- How many children your age can walk side by side across the clatter bridge? (*about 2*)

Elevations for many parts of the Sample Plan are shown. Ask your students these questions.

- For which piece of equipment are there 2 elevations? Why?

- What other parts of the structure might need two elevations to picture it completely?

- Describe what the platforms would look like from the side. (The elevation of each deck will be different depending on its height)

- The ramp, tire net, and chain net look similar from the top and from the side. Why? (*They go up from the ground to the deck at a 45° angle.*)

On another sheet of tracing paper, have students trace elevations for some parts of the structure from the elevation template, then answer the following questions using their Bodies in Space sheets for reference.

- Could a three-year-old stand under the tube slide? (*Some could, others might hit their head.*)

- How long are the chains on the ring trek? (*1 foot*) How far apart are the rungs of the ladder that lead up to it? (*1 foot*)

- What would be a good height for the chin bar for someone your age?

- How many 3-foot paces would it take to walk the length of the playground unit at the top of the Elevations Template? (*about 10*)

- How high is the peak on the roofed tower? (*11 feet*)

Have students put their worksheets, tracings, drawings, and pipe-cleaner figures in their design notebooks.

The Design Process

Students are introduced to the steps of the design process. They learn what makes a good playground plan.

Time. 30 minutes
Place. classroom

Materials

- transparencies of Sample Playgrounds 1–7
- transparencies of Sample Plan and Space Needs for Wheelchair Use
- transparencies of Plan Template and Elevation Template with pieces cut out
- easel with paper
- Evaluation, for reference
- Sample Site, for reference

per student

- design notebook
- $1\frac{1}{4}$-inch-tall toy figure (Lego® people) or 1-inch pipe-cleaner figure
- penny

Preparation

- Make or locate transparencies of Sample Playgrounds (pages 42–53), Sample Plan (page 38), Plan Template (page 39), Elevation Template (page 40), and Space Needs for Wheelchair Use (page 41). Have overhead projector ready to use.

- Cut out the pieces of the Plan Template and Elevation Template transparencies.

Sample Playgrounds

To facilitate the planning discussion, show the class transparencies of several sample playgrounds. For six of the seven sample playground plans (pages 41–51), there are photographs or perspective drawings; you might ask students to match each plan with its three dimensional image.

Sample 1, reproduced to the scale $\frac{1}{4}$ inch = 1 foot, is designed for children 3 to 6 years old. It is designed like a playhouse but also provides a slide and places to climb.

Sample 2 is reproduced to the scale $\frac{1}{4}$ inch = 1 foot and is designed for children 3 to 6 years old. It engages children's imaginations with tables, benches, and shelves. The advertisement describes it as, "a fine alternative to a more traditional playhouse."

Sample 3 is designed to accommodate 18 children ages 3 to 8. The structure is 23 feet 2 inches by 22 feet 6 inches and requires a space 36 feet square. The cost is $11,000.

Sample 4 is designed to accommodate 15 children ages 3 to 10. It requires a space 29 feet by 31 feet. If recycled plastic rather than wood is used for the decks, the cost is a little more than $7000 (add $300 for treated pine or $250 for redwood).

Sample 5 can accommodate 60 children ages 5 to 12. It requires a space 50 feet by 66 feet. The pieces weigh 7,786 pounds, and it will take 141 hours to install. The cost is about $25,000.

Sample 6 can accommodate 70 children ages 5 to 12. It requires a space 59 feet by 64 feet, weighs 9,235 pounds, and will take 150 hours to install.

Sample 7 will accommodate 140 children. Each numbered piece has a name. This plastic play structure can be assembled indoors or outdoors. It occupies a space 35 feet 4 inches by 40 feet 4 inches and is 15 feet 3 inches high. The cost of this two-level play structure is $164,000. Talk with your students about what the names tell you about the activities children can do on the Playrobics Maze.

As you talk about the play structures, use pieces of the Sample Plan, Plan Template, and Elevation Template transparencies to illustrate points in the discussion.

Have students use their Actions Lists (Activity 1), Bodies in Space (Activity 2), Children's Play Survey results (Activity 3), and Sample Plans (Activity 5) as they think and talk about playground design.

Discuss with students these design components.

1. Identify the design problem.

2. Think up possible solutions for that problem.

3. Choose one solution and draw the design.

4. Evaluate that solution.

5. Present and implement that solution.

Steps 1, 2, and 3 are introduced in this activity. Steps 4 and 5 are introduced in Activity 8.

Identifying the Design Problem

To identify the design problem, you have to answer questions such as these.

- Who will use the playground?

- What actions will they do there?

- In what types of spaces will they play?

- Where is the site? What are its natural features? What borders the site?

- Is the playground's layout a good one?

- How safe is the site?

- How dense is the site? How many children can safely play there?

- How much will it cost to build the playground?

The following text expands on these questions to help you lead a class discussion. Develop an easel list of key points from the discussion. Have students copy this list in their design notebooks and title it "Design Process."

Who. Who is the client (the person requesting the playground)? Who will use the playground? What are their ages and physical abilities? How many children can the playground accommodate?

Discuss why children of different ages might need different types of playground spaces. Children are different sizes (refer to Bodies in Space), have different physical abilities, require different safety factors, have various styles of playing, and so on.

Discuss ideas for playgrounds for handicapped children—playgrounds that are exciting, that can be negotiated independently, and that go well beyond the add-some-ramps solution. Display the Space Needs for Wheelchair Use transparency.

Ask students how they could make a playground accessible to a child in a wheelchair. Children in wheelchairs can spin and swing, for example, once they lock their chairs into place on a moveable platform. Low transfer platforms can provide entry and exit points, and bump stairs can be negotiated by wheelchairs. Rings set at a proper height can help children develop upper body strength, and activity panels within reach can certainly be enjoyed by all. Cushioned rubber matting is often used to give wheelchairs an accessible route of travel to and on the playground. The best special needs playgrounds are safe, integrated play areas that allow children of all abilities to share the same spaces. Show Sample Playground 5 again as an example.

Blind children can negotiate many standard playground pieces provided there are added safety features such as tunnel slides (instead of open slides) and higher railings on high platforms. Blind children can use tactile and sound clues to move through changeable mazes and can play communication games at sound stations.

What. What is the client's vision for the playground? What does the client expect the users will be able to do there? On which pieces can you do mainly one action? On which pieces can you do many different actions?

Will there be these types of spaces?

- open spaces, closed spaces

- high spaces, low spaces

- large gathering (theater) spaces

- small gathering (meeting, planning, hiding, refuge) spaces

- wet spaces, nature spaces

- building (sandbox) spaces, roadway spaces

- spinning spaces

- imaginative (adventure, fantasy, domestic play) spaces

Where. Where is the building site? Sites need not be flat, featureless, or rectangular. Using the Sample Site as a guide, draw a site on the chalkboard. Discuss how specific features might become places to play. The site may have a stream to jump across or to bridge; a shade tree for hiding, spying, or resting; a hill for stairs, ramps, or slides; and so on.

If the site is next to a busy road, it needs a fence. If it is next to a park or school, access to that site would be a good idea. Structures right next to school classroom windows create noise for students inside. Discuss good places for a playground on your school grounds.

Layout. To see the layout of a playground, envision the paths (traffic patterns) children might take as they move from one playground piece to another. A good layout allows for logical movement from space to space. A good layout is interesting, challenging, and full of choices.

Safety. Safe surfacing materials must be indicated on each plan. Playgrounds need either 12 inches of fine sand, 12 inches of pea gravel, 12 inches of wood mulch, resilient rubber cushioning, or a combination of these. A fall of more than 5 feet onto sand or gravel, or more than 8 feet onto wood mulch or rubber cushioning, is considered too dangerous.

Safe surfaces must extend 4 feet to 6 feet beyond all play pieces (see the Sample Plan). The front of slides must have a safety zone of at least 7 feet. Swings cannot be attached to a climbing structure and need a 9-foot zone.

Density. As the Bodies in Space activities showed, bodies take up space. Is there enough space between playground pieces for children to run without crashing into other children? Students can move pennies, laid flat, about on their Sample Plans to represent a 3-foot circle of space surrounding a moving child. If there is enough room for a penny to slide through a space, there is enough room for that child. When determining the number of children allowed on a playground, figure 70 square feet of play space for each child.

Cost. How much money is available for design, construction, and regular maintenance (monthly and yearly inspection and repairs) of the playground? The cost of a playground ranges from $10,000 to $70,000 or more depending upon size and type of equipment.

Making Pattern-Block Playgrounds

Students apply the design principles they learned in the previous activity as they create playground plans out of pattern blocks and other flat manipulatives.

Time. 45 minutes plus time for presentations (optional)

Place. classroom

Materials

per student

- at least one 11- by 17-inch sheet of $\frac{1}{4}$-inch grid paper (or two $8\frac{1}{2}$- by 11-inch sheets taped together)

- 1 penny or 1-inch scale figure

- 10 or more pattern blocks and other flat math manipulatives

- sharpened pencil

- drafting triangle, compass, and ruler

- design notebook

Directing the Activity

Give each student a piece of grid paper, one penny or scale figure (about 1 inch tall), and several good handfuls of flat math manipulatives. Pattern blocks, 1-inch math tiles, round poker chips, and small cardboard rectangles from board games work well. Explain that the paper is their site. In $\frac{1}{4}$ inch = 1 foot scale, establish the site's dimensions and area (square footage).

Ask students, "In this scale, what are the dimensions of a 1-inch math tile?" (*It is 4 feet by 4 feet.*) "What is a tile's area or square footage?" (*It is 16 square feet.*) Get out the square foot and discuss the relationship between the squares on the grid paper and squares in real life (such as a classroom's floor tiles). This is the time to develop this spatial sense. In future plans, you will often see students' tendency to crowd too much on one page. For example, they will draw slides that only a doll will fit down!

Explain to students that the manipulatives represent whatever playground pieces they wish to invent (as long as they can clearly explain its purpose). Have students arrange the manipulatives on the grid paper to represent a well-thought-out plan of a playground (looking down on it). Remind them to refer to the Design Process notes they made in the previous activity. Insist students use the manipulatives flat or on edge only, not stacked. They are working in plan here, not building three-dimensional structures.

Have students use the scale figures to establish a sense of scale. For example, how large should a platform be? How much space should there be between playground pieces?

Students will need to get the block layout and the drawing done in the time allotted. You may have to tell them, at some point, to stop playing and start drawing. Have students neatly trace (or draw with the help of rulers) their playgrounds, remove the manipulatives, and view their drawn plans. If students run out of manipulatives, have them trace some pieces, then pick them up and reuse them to continue their design.

Encourage students to name (label) each playground piece. They should also add a title block in one corner. The title block contains the title, the designer's name, and the scale, all in uniform block print.

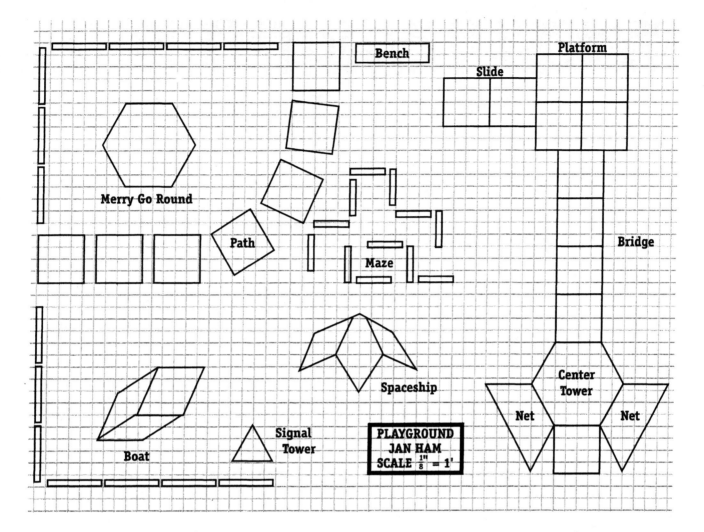

The pattern-block playground gives a two-dimensional view of the layout.

Finish the activity by having a few students present and explain their playground designs to the other students. Informally assess these drawings by referring to the Design Process notes. Each plan should clearly communicate the designer's ideas. You may want to take extra class time to have all students present their drawings. As an alternative, you could have students trade drawings to see if someone else can, using the manipulatives, accurately rebuild that playground according to the plan as drawn. Ask students to put their pattern-block plans in their design notebooks.

Evaluating a Playground

In this activity, students measure and draw a playground piece from a real playground. They draw the piece in plan and in elevation. Then they evaluate the playground using the Evaluation.

Time. two 45-minute sessions
Place. playground

Materials

- video camera (optional)

per team of 2 students

- measuring tape or yardstick

- drafting triangle, compass, and ruler

- several $8\frac{1}{2}$- by 11-inch sheets of $\frac{1}{4}$-inch grid paper

per student

- sharpened pencil

- design notebook

- clipboard

- Evaluation

Preparation

- Find a playground. Locate its original plan if possible.

- Make copies of Evaluation (pages 54–55).

Class Discussion

This activity helps students connect the playground structures they draw in scale with the dimensions of actual structures. The Survey Results easel list from Activity 3, which identifies behavior and location (what the child is playing and where), is a design tool to help in playground planning. Display this easel list and discuss it. Hand out the Evaluation and read through it with students, noting how it compares to their Design Process lists from Activity 6. Then divide the class into two-member teams.

Measuring and Drawing a Playground Piece

Have each team of students

- Measure and draw a scale plan of one playground piece or of one element of a play structure.

- Measure and draw a scale elevation of that piece.

- Include title block information—a title, designer's name, and the scale.

If you assign a different piece of equipment to each team, ensuring the whole playground gets drawn, you could later cut and paste the drawings together on a large sheet of paper for the class to study.

There is a lot of work here fitting the drawing onto the paper. Having extra grid paper available will help.

Remind students their plans and elevations should not look at all three-dimensional. The plans and elevations should be drawn on separate sheets of paper.

If you or some of your students make a video tour of the playground, you could use the video to teach next year's classes.

Evaluating the Playground

Do any of the playground pieces resemble counterparts in the natural world? Have students refer to the Actions Lists in their design notebooks.

Using the Evaluation as a guide, discuss the playground's users, actions, spaces, site, layout, and safety. Go through each question on the Evaluation, having students fill in their own Evaluations. Encourage students to remember each factor on the Evaluation. They will be applying these factors in future work. Here's how students' design notebook materials relate to the factors on the Evaluation.

- All the factors relate to the Design Process list.

- *Who* relates to Bodies in Space, Children's Play Survey, and the Survey Results list.

- *What* relates to the Actions List and the Children's Play Survey.

- *Where* relates to the Actions List and the Sample Site.

- *Layout* relates to the tracings of the Sample Plan.

- *Density* relates to Bodies in Space, String Math, and the pattern-block playground plan.

The factors on the Evaluation come up again as students design contracts in the next activity and as they do their final projects.

Use specific examples as you discuss your playground, and encourage students to do the same.

"The end of this slide is 8 feet from this tire ladder. Is that safe enough?"

"You say ten-year-olds would like the tower. What might they play there, and how many can fit in the tower?"

"What pieces from your pattern-block playgrounds were the same (in-scale) shape and size as this platform?"

Ask students how they might improve the playground. What they would add, modify, or take away, and why? Have students save their plan drawings, elevation drawings, and Evaluations in their design notebooks.

Designing from Contracts

In this activity, each student fills out a contract for design specifications of a playground. Students design sample playgrounds using traced templates or ideas of their own, then estimate the costs of their proposals. Designs are reviewed by other students.

Time. two 45-minute sessions
Place. classroom

Materials

- transparency of Contract

per student

- Contract

- Plan Template and Elevation Template

- sheet of 11- by 17-inch tracing paper

- sharpened pencil

- drafting triangle, compass, and ruler

- scale figure or penny

- drafting tape

- design notebook

Preparation

- Make copies of Contract (page 56), Plan Template (page 39), and Elevation Template (page 40).

- Make a transparency of Contract. Have an overhead projector ready to use.

- Post the easel list Design Process created in Activity 6.

Class Discussion

Review the Design Process list with students. Discuss the decisions to be made when building a playground. Students need to decide what actions they will allow for (such as running and sliding), what spaces they will specify (such as open and closed), and so on. Tell students they will design from specifications written on a contract they create.

Writing the Contract

Use the Contract transparency to guide students through filling out a sample contract. Students should recognize the Contract's factors—they are used on the Evaluation. Limit the number of actions, spaces, and layouts students can design from. For example, allow six actions, three spaces, and two layouts. Hand out a Contract to each student. Tell students they can be their own clients or may invent clients' names. (See page 30 for some creative names for which students could build unusual playgrounds.)

Drawing the Site

Have students design sites on 11- by 17-inch tracing paper by tracing the hill, stream, and trees from the Sample Site anywhere on their tracing papers.

Creating the Design

Have students trace parts from the Plan Template or Sample Plan to create a playground. They can add ideas of their own if those ideas are properly scaled and drawn. Be sure students include title block information: a title, their name, and the scale. Remind them to use scale figures or pennies to maintain a sense of scale. Ask students to save the templates in their design notebooks.

Figuring the Cost

Have students do a cost analysis of their proposed playgrounds. Have them include initial site cost and taxes if you wish. Here is a sample.

Design cost
(planning, design, consulting)......$1,000
Figure square footage of entire
    playground area
    (44 feet by 68 feet = 2992 feet^2)
Structures
    ($10.00 to $15.00 per square foot
    of playground)
    for example, $12 x 2992 feet^2......$35,904
Shipping (4 percent of structures' cost) . $1400
Three-Year Maintenance Contract.....$600
    Total.......................$37,904

Adjust this part of the lesson to a level most suited to your students' mathematical capabilities, or omit this step and announce there are no cost constraints.

Students must be sure they meet all the planning requirements. They should do a second draft if necessary.

Reviewing the Plans

Have the designers trade their completed contracts, playground drawings, and cost analyses with another student (the reviewer). Using an Evaluation as reference, the reviewer must evaluate the plan. Is the design a good one? The reviewer can ask the designer to explain or defend the design. If the design is inadequate or incomprehensible, the reviewer can offer suggestions for improvements and ask the designer to resubmit a modified plan.

When a plan receives a favorable review, designers present their plans to you or to a student safety committee for approval. (See page 60 for a list of publications on public playground safety.)

Have students put their contracts, approved drawings, and cost analyses in their design notebooks.

Three-Dimensional Models

In this activity, students cut, fold, and tape triangle paper and grid paper to make three-dimensional playground models. An art teacher would be a welcomed partner here as students are joining the mathematics of shapes to the realm of paper sculptures.

Time. 45 minutes

Place. classroom

Materials

- transparency of Triangle Paper
- transparency of $\frac{1}{4}$-Inch Grid Paper

per team of 2 students

- several sheets of Triangle Paper
- several $8\frac{1}{2}$- by 11-inch sheets of $\frac{1}{4}$-inch grid paper
- scissors
- tape and glue (stick or liquid)
- scale figures
- string (optional)

Preparation

- Make copies of Triangle Paper (page 58), preferably on various colors of card stock. If you have access to an enlarging copier machine, make two or three sizes of triangles. For example, create 1-inch, 1.5-inch, and 2-inch triangles.

- Build sample structures to show students.
  Fold three triangles into a tetrahedron with one open face to serve as a cave.
  Cut strips of triangles for paths or for a slide.
  Make a merry-go-round using hexagons from two sizes of triangles.

  Use a square pyramid as part of a climbing structure.
  Combine hexagons and triangles into climbing structures.

- Make a transparency of Triangle Paper and $\frac{1}{4}$-Inch Grid Paper. Have an overhead projector ready to use.

- Clear a large table for display.

Working with Triangles

Pass out several sheets of triangle paper, scissors, tape, and glue to two-student design teams. As a class, discuss how triangles join to make rhombuses, trapezoids, and hexagons. (See page 27.) Trace these shapes on the Triangle Grid transparency. The diagram on the next page shows some examples of how to cut the Triangle Paper to make different shapes. The dotted line indicates a fold; the heavy line indicates an edge that will be taped to another edge.

Have teams cut out two, then three, then four connected triangles and see what three-dimensional sculptures they can make. Hold up some of the sculptures. Ask "If this were a one-quarter inch equals one foot scale model of some type of new playground sculpture, what might that structure be?"

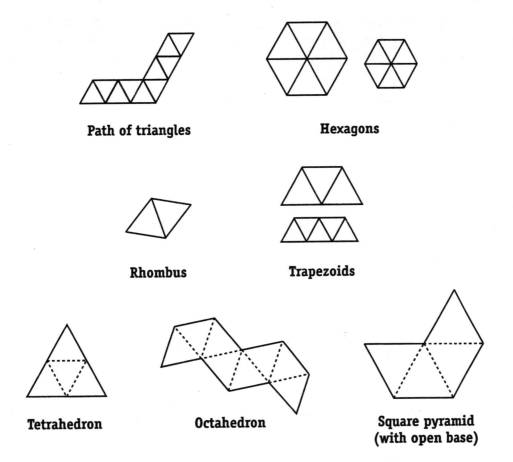

Path of triangles

Hexagons

Rhombus

Trapezoids

Tetrahedron

Octahedron

**Square pyramid
(with open base)**

Continue to have the teams cut, fold, and tape combinations of adjoining triangles into three-dimensional shapes. Have them use the scale figures to help imagine what that shape could be. Ask questions such as, "Can a person hide inside this space?" "Can a child reach to climb this structure?"

Teams may create some two-dimensional shapes such as a hexagon as a spinning platform and a series of triangles as stepping stones. But encourage teams to keep experimenting with the more difficult three-dimensional shapes.

Sharing ideas between groups is a good idea here. Students will be challenged to recreate other teams' models.

At some point someone will ask, "Can't we use other materials?" You can say no, the challenge is to see what can be developed with the materials at hand, or yes, but only string. String itself has some geometric validity (it makes a line) and is a necessary part of many playground pieces (trolleys, swings, bridges, nets, and so on).

Use the geometric terms for the shapes students create. Are students aware that they have used hexagons, tetrahedrons, or octahedrons?

Working with Squares

Pass out several sheets of grid paper to the teams. Working with squares usually leads to more common-place playground pieces. While still giving the teams the freedom to invent unique sculptures, suggest they also make a few conventional playground pieces such as square raised platforms, slides, bridges, and jungle gyms.

As you did with the triangle transparency, use the grid-paper transparency to show students specific combinations of blocks to cut and fold.

Students may ask how to support their structures. Help teams discover some basic structural truths.

- Turning a strip of paper into a box beam or, even better, a cylinder will make a good supporting post.

- Reinforcing the diagonal of a square with a triangle makes it stronger. When you notice students trying to support sagging structures, discuss how triangles and squares may need to work together (as in truss bridges).

Ask students to compare the triangle-based sculptures to the square-based ones. Why are they so different? How many sides does it take of each to make an enclosed space?

Could any good models be made by somehow combining triangle and square pieces together (for example, a pyramidal roof for a square structure)?

Creating the Super Sculpture Playground

Have each team choose several of its best triangle and square sculptures to be placed in a super sculpture playground arranged on a large display table. Each piece must have a name—conventional or invented (the octa-spinning hedron, the monster masher)—describing what type of playground piece it represents.

Ask the class for ideas on how to lay out the playground on its site. If you try being more of an observer and less of a participant in this discussion, you will hear students debating points from previous activities. For example, they may talk about who may use the playground, what types of spaces are being created, whether there is enough space between the pieces, and whether the layout is challenging and full of choices.

Have students arrange the sculptures on the table. Grant requests for site improvements if you so desire—green paper for grass, blue for water, black for roadways—and your super sculpture playground is complete.

Extensions. The designers may become quite attached to their creations. They may want to modify it over the days to come or have you leave it up for a very long time. This is natural part of creating; don't discourage it. The following activities extend the usefulness of the display.

- Add scale buildings to the site.

- Photograph the display or draw parts of it.

- Have students evaluate the playground using the Evaluation.

- Invent a setting for the playground. What town is it in? What is nearby? Bring the scale figures to life and write stories using the playground as the setting.

Final Project

Through this activity, students show how many of the skills taught thus far have become a real part of their designing. Final project grades are based on the Evaluation factors.

Time. two 45-minute sessions plus 30 minutes for class presentations

Place. classroom and at home

Materials

per student

- Final Project
- Evaluation
- Contract
- model-building materials
- design notebooks
- several 11- by 17-inch sheets of tracing paper
- several 11- by 17-inch sheets of $\frac{1}{4}$-inch grid paper
- sharpened pencil
- drafting triangle, compass, ruler

Preparation

- Make copies of Final Project (page 57), Contract (page 56), and Evaluation (pages 54–55).

- Have students start early in gathering model-building materials. See the list on page 3 for ideas.

- Arrange a class exhibit for the plans and projects and invite parents, the school, and the community.

- Consider inviting an architect to serve on the Review Committee.

Class Discussion

Explain to students that for their final projects, they will be handling all aspects of designing and building a playground model. Remind students to use the wealth of planning information in their design notebooks. They will need to be able to justify why they designed what they did the way they did. Some elements from earlier student plans may be incorporated into a new design, but this is supposed to be just that—a new design. If students have trouble with this project, it may be because their designs are too complicated. A simple project, done well, is better than a complicated, confusing one.

Give students the choice of working alone or in two-member design teams. Some work will be done at home, so team members will have to be able to meet together outside of class.

Tasks for the Final Project

1. Students will submit a contract stating who the client is, who the users of the playground will be, what actions and spaces it will feature, where the playground will be located, and how much money will be spent on the project. Students can be their own clients, or they can invent a client. Here are a few ideas.

I. M. Spooky—a haunted house

Dolly Finn—a water park

King Minos—a labyrinth-based playground

T. Worthington Green—a super miniature golf course

Hansel and Gretel—an edible playground model

Swiss Family Robinson—a playground with a tree house in the center

Mrs. Crittersby—a playground for otters, monkeys, or other playful animals

A. Lee N.—a low-gravity playground or a no-gravity playground

To completely carry out the idea of a playground for animals or aliens, students would need to do extra background research on how these other creatures play and on how much space they would need. If you want all your students to create play spaces for children, don't suggest nonhuman clients. Some of your very creative students may be willing to put in the extra effort to research and describe the play, safety, and space needs of other creatures and then design a suitable playground.

Review and approve each student's contract before they continue.

2. Students create a site plan noting site dimensions and geographic features. Remind them that although paper is rectangular, their sites do not have to be rectangular.

3. Students draw a first sketch on their sites to establish layout, scale, and what spaces might be next to what.

4. Students use the Evaluation to assess their own work. Is the design planned with the client, users, actions, and site in mind? How can it be improved?

Go over the sketches with each student. You need to be sure they are on track at this point. Some students will realize that much of their plan needs redoing. To reduce the frustration of starting over, encourage students to use tracing paper to modify sketches and improve neatness.

5. Students need to gather suitable model-building materials before making the final drawing. It is easier to adapt a drawing to accommodate found materials than it is to start with a final drawing and then attempt to find materials of specific shapes and sizes.

6. Students do a final drawing complete with a title block and proper scale. Traced final drawings should be acceptable.

7. Students work at home to make models of their playgrounds.

8. Students present the final drawings and models to the class. You may choose to have the principal or an architect sit in on these presentations as part of a Review Committee.

Assessment

A successful final project will include the following.

- approved contract
- site plan
- first sketch
- student self-evaluation of that first sketch
- final drawing
- model
- presentation of the project to the class

The Contract, Evaluation, and Final Project worksheets clearly state what is expected of students. Use the Evaluation as your assessment tool, or develop your own grading criteria based on that worksheet.

The model is not graded by itself, since model-making skills were not a major part of this book, and students vary in their access to parental help and materials. Make very clear that models are graded only on how well they relate to the plans. A great plan and a simple student-built model will receive a higher grade than a mediocre plan and a lavish, professional-looking model.

Recalling the discussion of architectural design education in this book's introduction may help you assess the effectiveness of the playground design project as a whole. How well did students develop and use a process of design, make connections between disciplines, solve open-ended problems, and work cooperatively in design teams? Did they create, control, and make good decisions about their built environment? Did they use the technology and art of design to clearly express their ideas?

What Actions?

Use your Actions List to help you list at least 3 actions that could be done on each of these man-made play structures. Give the structure a name.

Title _____
Actions _____

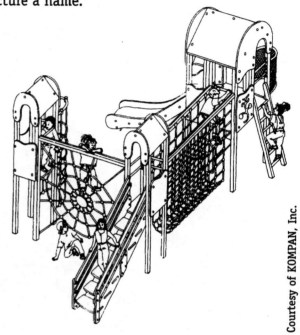

Title _____
Actions _____

Title _____
Actions _____

Imagine play equipment called Hamster Wheel. Talk about or draw your ideas. Do the same for these other names.

    Mini-Mountain
    Springboard
    Sky Flight
    Turntable
    Tilted Train
    Curling Arch Climber
    Secret Tunnel
    Sound Tube
    Giant Water Maze

Bodies in Space

This chart shows the size of a typical 3-year old—the child's height, reach, and so on.

Measure someone your age. Round off to the nearest half a foot.

height _____   width of body _____   arm-spread _____

sitting, seat height _____   sitting, head height _____

one pace _____   one running pace _____   one long jump _____

space to crawl through _____   height _____   width _____

height to step _____   height to reach _____

On a piece of grid paper, draw stick figures to accurately represent the above measurements. Each block on the grid paper represents 1 foot.

1. How long and wide would a bridge be for two 3-year-olds to cross, side-by-side, in 5 paces? _____

2. Add 1 foot to your reach to determine how high off of the ground monkey bars should be for someone your age. _____

3. What are the dimensions of the smallest square your entire class could fit in, standing comfortably?   Estimate _____   Measurement _____

4. What is the diameter of the largest circle your entire class could make, standing fingertip to fingertip?   Estimate _____   Measurement _____

5. Could someone your age comfortably crawl through an 18-inch diameter pipe? _____

Children's Play Survey

Date _____

Observer _____ **Subjects** _____

Observe one subject for 5 minutes.

Mark in the boxes below what actions the subject is doing or in what space he or she is playing.

Mark **B** if your subject is a boy, **G** if your subject is a girl.

Balance	Fall	Jump	Seek	Yell
Build/Dig	Fight	Pretend	Slide	_____
Chase	Fly	Rest	Spin	_____
Climb	Get Wet	Ride	Swing	_____
Crawl	Hang	Roll	Talk	_____
Cross	Hide	Run	Watch/Spy	_____

String Math

Make a 12-square by 12-square grid outside on your playground. Each square will be 1 foot by 1 foot.

1. What is the perimeter of the whole grid? _____ feet
   What is the area of the grid? _____ square feet
   What is the length of the diagonal of the grid _____ feet

2. How many paces would it take to walk the diagonal of the grid?
   Estimate _____ Measurement _____

Use chalk and string to draw the following shapes on your outdoor grid. Each $\frac{1}{4}$-inch square block on this page will equal a 1-by-1-foot square of real space on your outdoor grid. These drawings are done as if looking straight down from above.

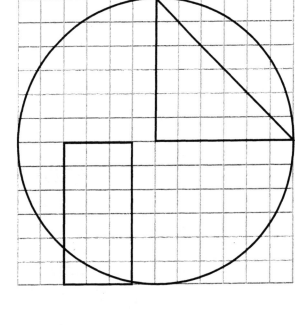

3. What is the radius of the circle? _____
   How does the length of the radius compare with length of one side of the square? _____

4. How many of the small triangles would fit inside of the whole grid? _____
   How many children you age could comfortably fit inside the small triangle? _____
   How many children your are could comfortably fit inside of the whole grid? _____

5. If the rectangle, triangle, and circle were pieces of a playground plan which shape do you think would be:

   a pool _____
   a platform _____
   a bridge or slide _____

Sample Site

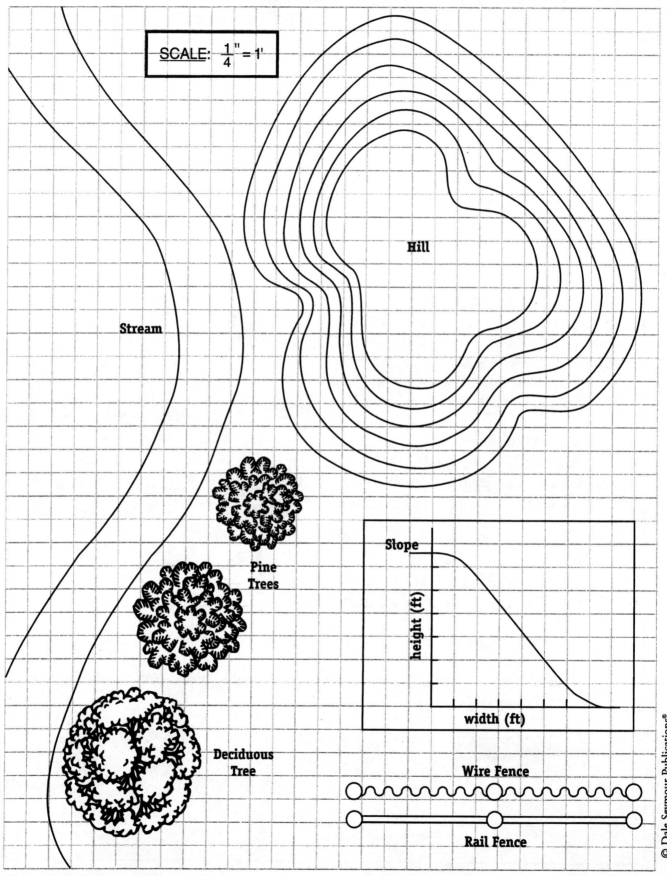

SCALE: $\frac{1}{4}'' = 1'$

Hill

Stream

Pine Trees

Slope

height (ft)

width (ft)

Deciduous Tree

Wire Fence

Rail Fence

From Perspective to Plan

Here is a perspective drawing of a playground. All of the pieces of this playground are drawn below in plan view. Cut out each piece and assemble an accurate plan of the playground.

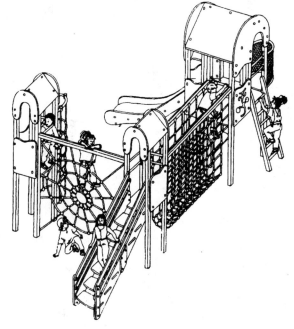

Courtesy of KOMPAN, Inc.

Circle Net (spider web)

Slide

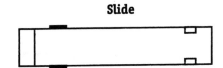

Tower Net

Ladder

Large Tower

Tower Net

Small Tower

Small Tower

Staircase

Net bridge

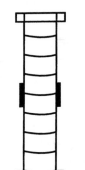

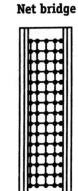

SCALE: $\frac{1}{4}" = 1'$

Sample Plan

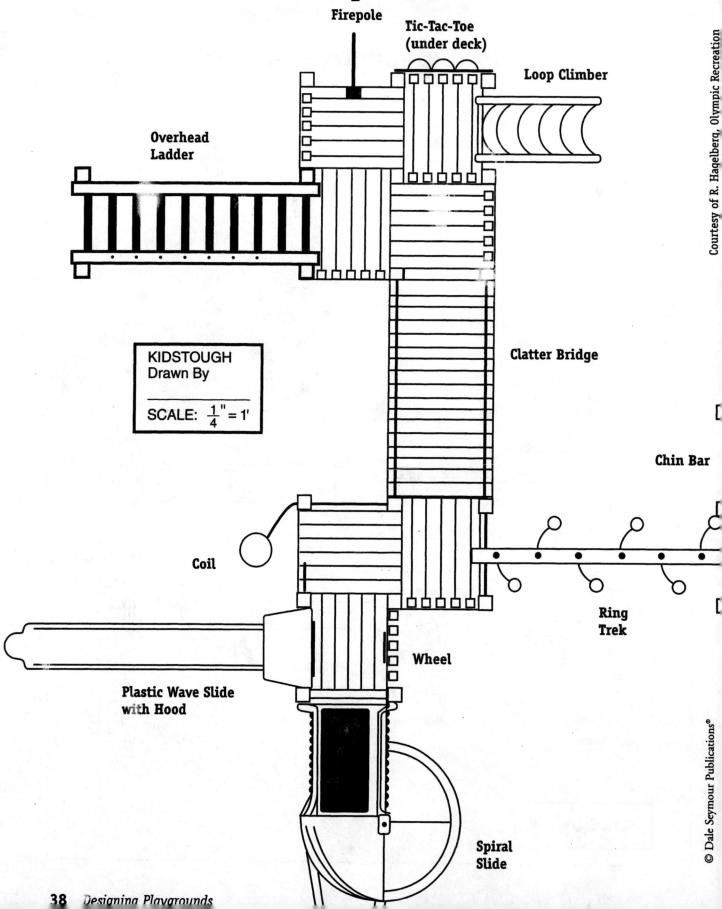

Firepole

Tic-Tac-Toe
(under deck)

Loop Climber

Overhead
Ladder

Clatter Bridge

KIDSTOUGH
Drawn By

SCALE: $\frac{1}{4}$" = 1'

Chin Bar

Coil

Wheel

Ring
Trek

Plastic Wave Slide
with Hood

Spiral
Slide

Courtesy of R. Hagelberg, Olympic Recreation

© Dale Seymour Publications®

Plan Template

SCALE: $\frac{1}{4}" = 1'$

Spiral Slide

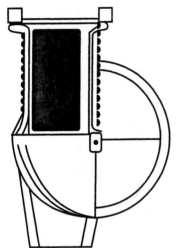

Chain Net

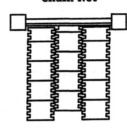

Ring Trek

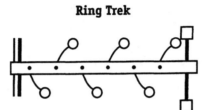

Sandbox

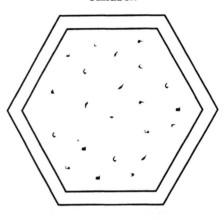

Tire Net

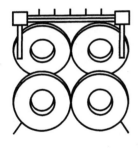

Tunnel

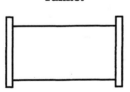

Clatter Bridge

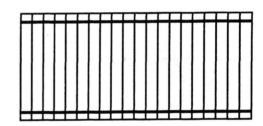

Coil

Firepole

Ladder

Tube Slide

Wheel

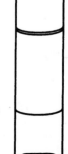

Tire Swing

17'

Elevation Template

SCALE: $\frac{1}{4}'' = 1'$

Chain Net

Tube Slide

Tire Net

Access Ladder

Chin Bar

6'

Ring Trek

Ring Trek

Coil

Firepole

Space Needs for Wheelchair Use

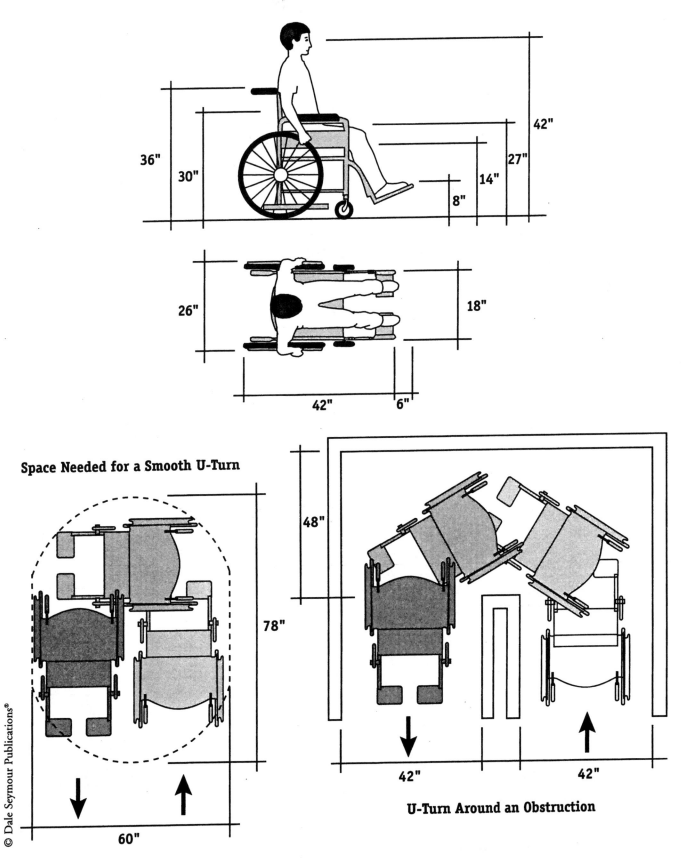

36"

30"

42"

27"

14"

8"

26"

18"

42"

6"

Space Needed for a Smooth U-Turn

48"

78"

60"

42"

42"

U-Turn Around an Obstruction

Sample Playground 1

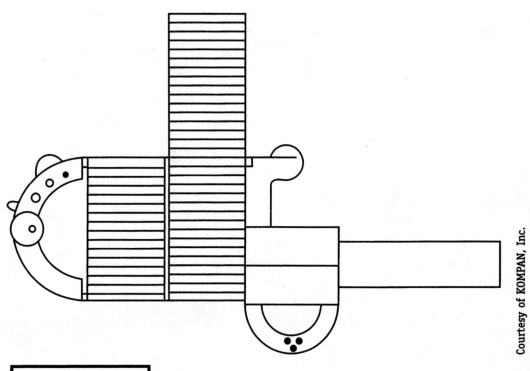

SCALE: $\frac{1}{4}$" = 1'

Courtesy of KOMPAN, Inc.

Sample Playground 2

Courtesy of KOMPAN, Inc.

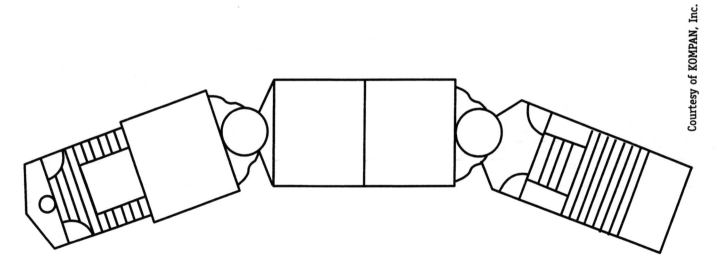

SCALE: $\frac{1}{4}$" = 1'

Sample Playground 3

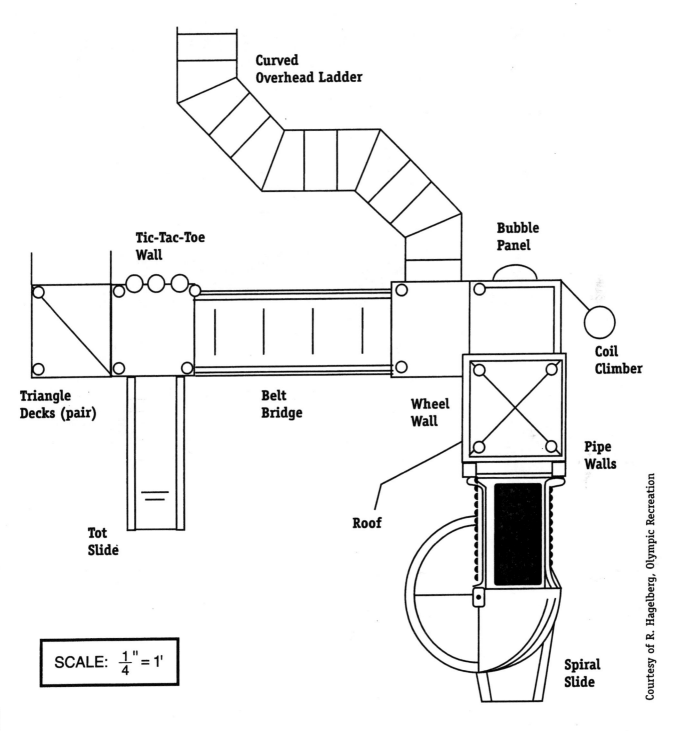

Curved
Overhead Ladder

Tic-Tac-Toe
Wall

Bubble
Panel

Coil
Climber

Triangle
Decks (pair)

Belt
Bridge

Wheel
Wall

Pipe
Walls

Tot
Slide

Roof

Spiral
Slide

SCALE: $\frac{1}{4}$ " = 1'

Courtesy of R. Hagelberg, Olympic Recreation

Sample Playground 4

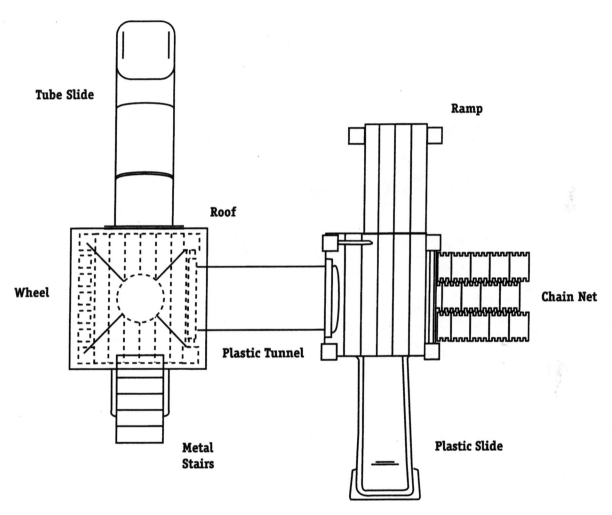

Tube Slide

Ramp

Roof

Wheel

Chain Net

Plastic Tunnel

Metal
Stairs

Plastic Slide

Courtesy of R. Hagelberg, Olympic Recreation

SCALE: $\frac{1}{4}$" = 1'

Sample Playground 5

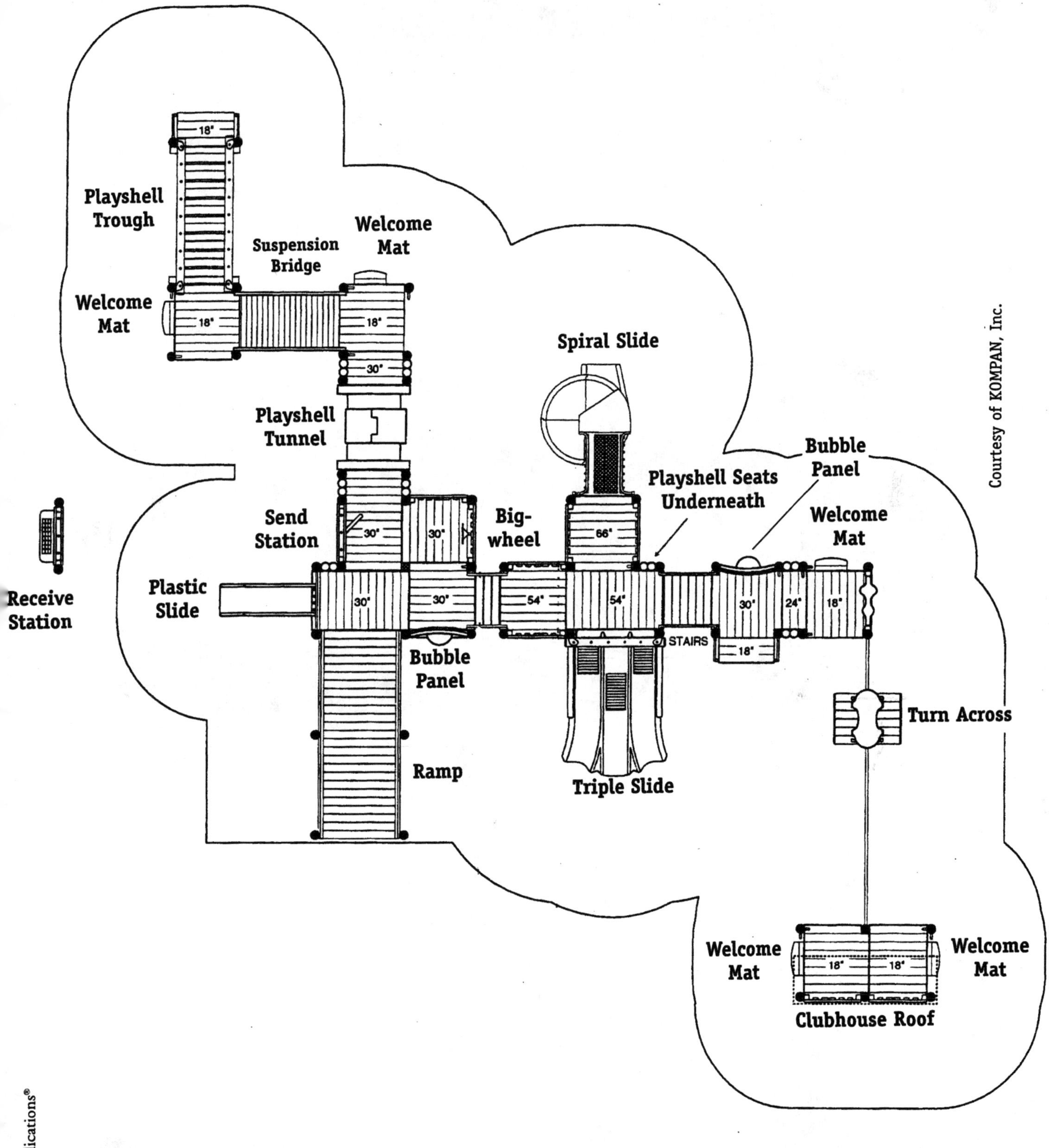

Playshell
Trough

Welcome
Mat

18"

Suspension
Bridge

Welcome
Mat

18"

18"

30"

Playshell
Tunnel

Spiral Slide

Bubble
Panel

Send
Station

30"

30"

Big-
wheel

66"

Playshell Seats
Underneath

Welcome
Mat

Receive
Station

Plastic
Slide

30"

30"

54"

54"

30"

24"

18"

STAIRS

18"

Bubble
Panel

Turn Across

Ramp

Triple Slide

Welcome
Mat

18"

18"

Welcome
Mat

Clubhouse Roof

Courtesy of KOMPAN, Inc.

SCALE: $\frac{1}{8}" = 1'$

Sample Playground 6

Courtesy of KOMPAN, Inc.

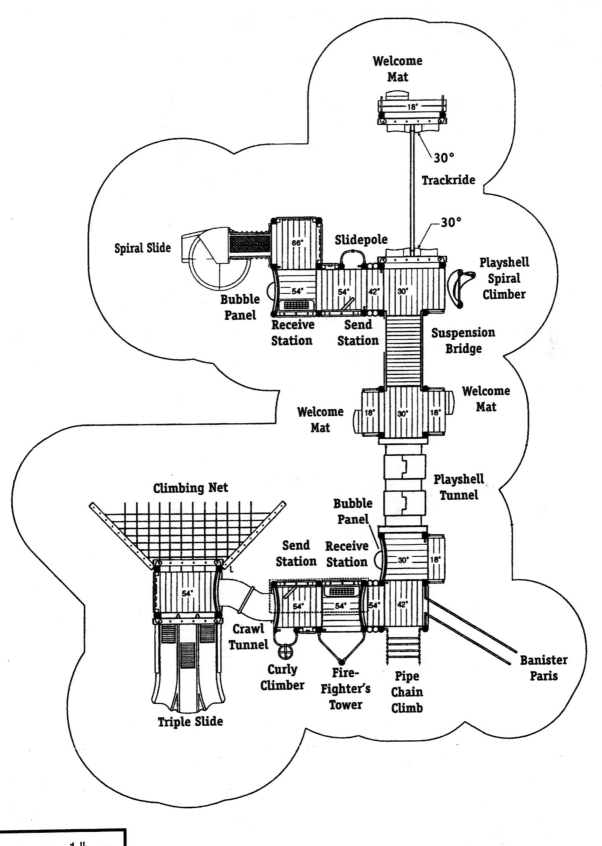

Welcome Mat

18"

30°

Trackride

30°

Spiral Slide

66"

Slidepole

Bubble Panel

54"

54" 42" 30"

Playshell Spiral Climber

Receive Station

Send Station

Suspension Bridge

Welcome Mat

18" 30° 18"

Welcome Mat

Climbing Net

Playshell Tunnel

Bubble Panel

Send Station

Receive Station

30° 18"

54"

54" 54" 54" 42"

Crawl Tunnel

Curly Climber

Fire-Fighter's Tower

Pipe Chain Climb

Banister Paris

Triple Slide

SCALE: $\frac{1"}{8} = 1'$

Sample Playground 7

Level 1

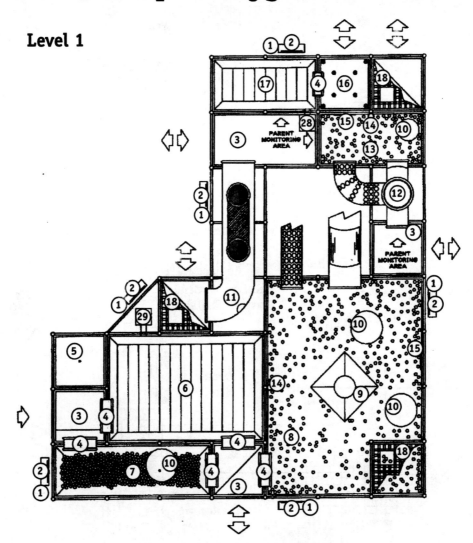

Courtesy of Pentes Play, Inc., Charlotte, North Carolina

PLAYROBICS MAZE

1. Shoe Cubby
2. Signage
3. Entry/Exit Pad
4. Entry/Exit Tube
5. Fireman's Pole Landing
6. Air Bounce
7. V Ball Slog
8. Ball Bath
9. King of the Mountain
10. Activity Ball
11. Monkey Maze

LITTLE KIDS AREA

12. Micro Junction with Dome, Slide, and U Tube
13. Baby Ball Bath
14. Ball Hoop
15. Target
16. Snake Trees
17. Air Hoop

Level 2

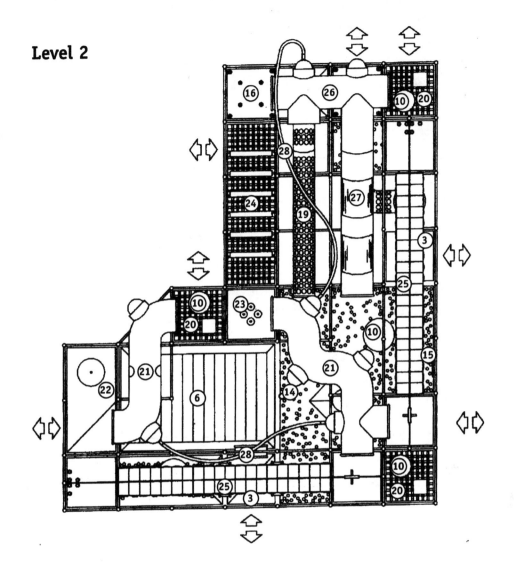

Courtesy of Pentes Play, Inc., Charlotte, North Carolina

TRANSITION AND UPPER LEVEL

18. Web Tower Entry

19. Tube Pull

20. Web Tower

21. Snake Crawl with Observation Domes

22. Fireman's Pole

23. Bumper Bags

24. Tube Jam

25. Trolley Slide

26. Junction Tube with Observation Dome

27. Super Slide with Port Lites

28. Tube Phone

29. Air Bounce Blower Motor

Evaluation

Project Title _____

Designer _____ **Evaluated by** _____

Part 1: The Playground

Who

1. Does the playground meet the needs of the client?
2. Does the playground meet the needs of the users?
3. What are the ages and abilities of the users?

What

4. Does the plan include places to do the actions specified in the contract?
5. What actions will the users do on the playground?
6. Does the plan include the spaces specified in the contract?
7. What types of spaces will the playground include?

Where

8. Does the plan use the site well?
9. Does it indicate the site's dimensions?

Layout

10. Does the layout meet the criteria specified in the contract? (logical, interesting, full of choices, challenging but safe)

Safety

11. Are safe surfacing materials indicated?
12. Is there 4 feet to 6 feet of safe surface beyond all play pieces?
13. Do slides have safety zone of 7 feet? Do swings have a 9-foot safety zone?
14. Are swings separated from other play structures?

Density

15. Allowing 70 square feet of play space per child, how many children could use this playground at one time?

Cost

16. Has a cost analysis proven that this playground can be built for the contracted price?

Suggestions

17. How could the playground be improved?

Part II: The Plan

1. Does the plan clearly communicate the designer's intent as detailed in the contract?
2. Is the plan neatly drawn? Does the plan show proper use of drawing tools?
3. Does the plan include a title block and labels?

Scale

4. Is the scale of the plan clearly indicated?
5. Does the overall scale of the plan make sense?
6. Does the size of each drawn playground piece make sense?

Model

7. How well does the model relate to the plan?

   - All model pieces are sized and placed to exactly match plan.
   - Most model pieces are sized and placed to match plan.
   - Model pieces and placement do not match plan.

Presentation

8. How well were the plan and model presented?

Contract

_____ Design Co. will design the playground

described herein for (client) _____ , to be used

by (users) _____ of ages _____ with abilities _____ .

The playground will be designed so that these actions can be performed there.

_____

It will include these types of spaces.

_____

The playground, to be built on the site described as _____ ,

will be of a layout that is

_____ logical   _____ interesting   _____ full of choices   _____ challenging but safe

It will comply with all current safety specifications and standards, including the use of

_____ as a surfacing material.

The playground plan will be completed by (date) _____

for a fee of $ _____ .

_____   _____
Design Co. Signature(s)   **Client Signature**

Date _____   Date _____

Final Project

Your project must include a scale plan and a model that relates well to that plan. You may include an elevation of part of your playground if you wish. You may work on your own, or in two-person design teams. A team may submit one model, but each student of that team must submit a drawing of the team's playground design. Record the due dates and check off the following tasks as you complete them.

Date due   Completed

_____ 1. Submit a contract. Get approval before going on.   _____

_____ 2. Do a site plan.   _____

_____ 3. Do a first sketch on that site.   _____

_____ 4. Informally evaluate that sketch and decide how it
             can be improved.   _____

_____ 5. Gather usable model-making materials.   _____

_____ 6. Do a final drawing that clearly communicates your playground
             ideas, complete with title block, labels, and proper use of scale.
             The final drawing can be on grid paper or tracing paper.   _____

_____ 7. Make a model.   _____

_____ 8. Present the contract, final drawing, and model to the
             Review Committee for evaluation.   _____

You may be your own client and design a playground for your school, for handicapped children, for younger children, or for another group. Or, you may invent a client.

Triangle Paper

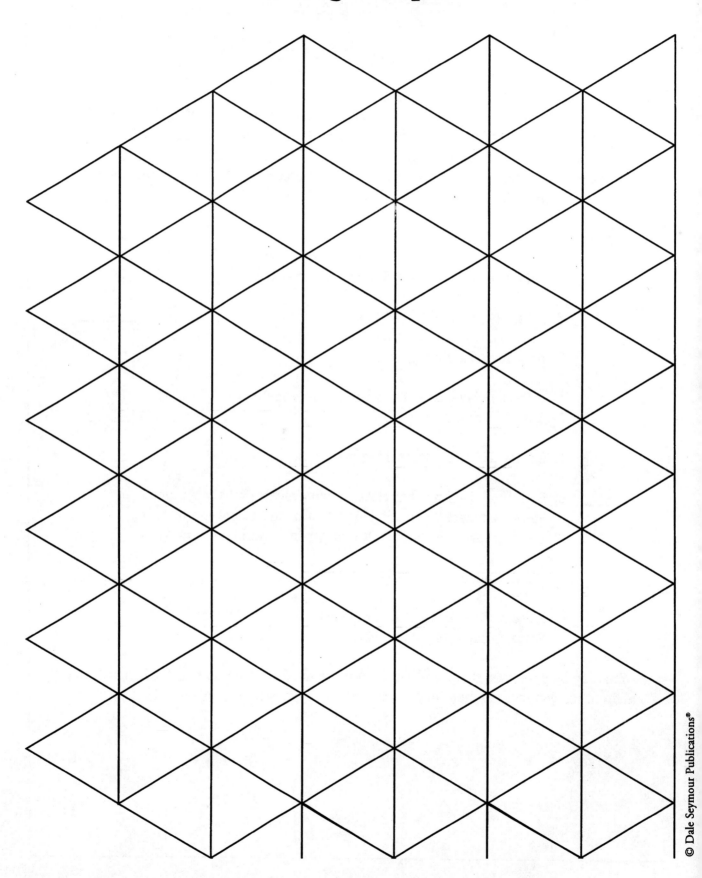

$\frac{1}{4}$-Inch Grid Paper

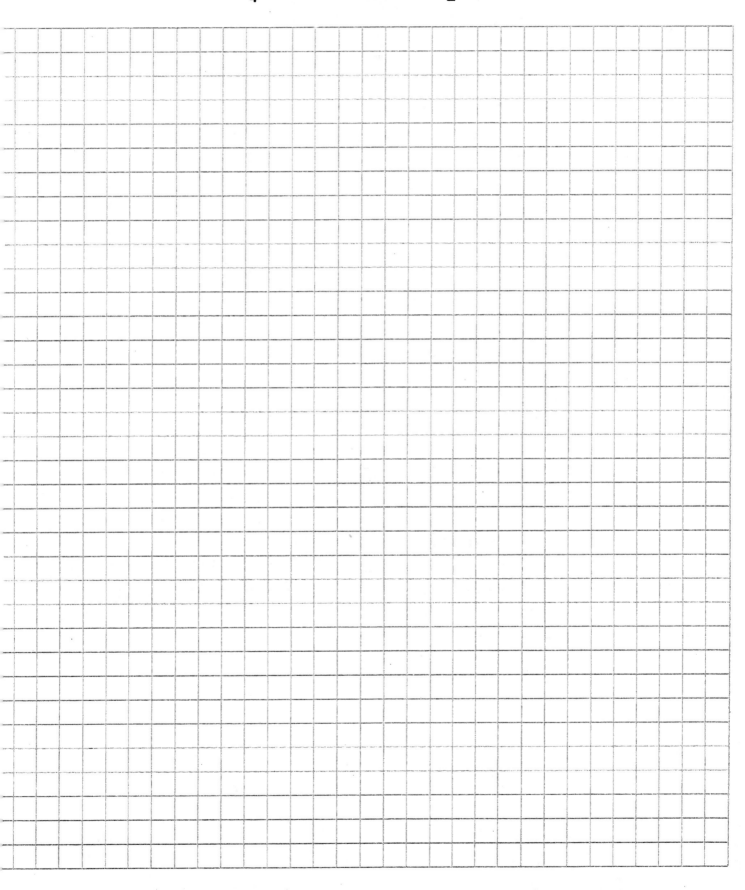

◆◇ RESOURCES ◇◆

Frost, J. L., and B. L. Klein. *Children's Play and Playgrounds.* Needham Heights, Mass.: Allyn & Bacon, 1983.

Senda, Mitsuru. *Design of Children's Play Environments.* New York: McGraw-Hill, 1992.

Related Books

Adkins, Jan. *The Art and Industry of Sandcastles.* New York: Walker, 1991.

Fulton, Brad, and Bill Lombard. *A Blueprint for Geometry.* Menlo Park, Calif.: Dale Seymour Publications, 1998.

Kirby, MaryAnn. "Nature as Refuge in Children's Environments," *Children's Environments Quarterly,* Vol. 6, No. 1 (Spring 1989) 7–12.

Nabhan, Gary P., and Stephen Trimble. *The Geography of Childhood: Why Children Need Wild Places.* Boston: Beacon Press, 1995.

Books about Structure

Salvadori, Mario. *The Art of Construction.* Chicago: Chicago Review Press, 1990.

Pollard, Jeanne. *Building Toothpick Bridges.* Palo Alto, Calif.: Dale Seymour Publications, 1985.

Zubrowski, Bernie. *Messing Around with Drinking Straw Construction.* New York: Little, Brown and Co., 1981.

Architectural Design Education Resources

Architecture and Children. The University of New Mexico, School of Architecture and Planning, 2414 Central S.E., Albuquerque, NM 87131-1226

Architecture in Education. The Foundation for Architecture, One Penn Center at Suburban Station, Philadelphia, PA 19103

Center for Understanding the Built Environment (CUBE). 5328 W. 67 Street, Prairie Village, Kansas 66208

About Playground Safety and Determining Equipment Dimensions

Guidelines for Public Playgrounds (US Consumer Product Safety Commission) Washington, DC 20207

Ramsey, Charles, and Harold Sleeper. *Architectural Graphic Standards,* The American Institute of Architects. New York: John Wiley and Sons, 1994.